C000203100

THE VERDERER'S VISION;
OR THE EPPING HAMADRYAD'S APPEAL.

The Verderer's Vision. *Punch*, 14 April 1894. Drawn by Linley Sambourne. The Corporation of
London, when they had saved the Forest, were frequently accused of vandalism through
their policy of removing poor specimens of trees, and particularly, of felling pollard
hornbeams. The axeman wears the Corporation's badge, and would have reminded the
Punch reader of Gladstone, whose hobby, famously, was felling trees.

WALKS IN LOUGHTON'S
FOREST

Short Epping Forest walks in and around Loughton
and historical notes on them
Illustrated with nineteenth century engravings

Second Edition

by Chris and Caroline Pond

Loughton
Published by the Loughton and District Historical Society
2007

Copies may be had by post
from the LDHS at Forest Villa, Staples Rd, Loughton, Essex, IG10 1HP.

First edition 2002
Reprinted 2003, 2005(twice)
Reprinted with minor corrections 2006
Second edition, 2007

©2002-2007: C & C Pond

ISBN-13: 978-1-905269-06-8

The illustrations are taken from the authors' collection. Where not specifically attributed, they are generally from the various editions of *Walks in Epping Forest*, by the Loughton author, Percy Lindley, 1884-1896. Cover picture – December Dawn on Staples Hill – *Chris Pond*

Printed in Great Britain by Joshua Horgan, Oxford

Contents

Maps

The maps are reproduced by kind permission of the Field Studies Council, Epping Forest Centre, from whom a publication reproducing all the maps to James Brimble's *London's Epping Forest* can be obtained.

The scale is shown on all the maps. Distances mentioned in the text are those that you can expect to traverse, rather greater than a straight line on a map, because of winding paths, detours to avoid muddy patches and fallen trees, etc.

Looking from Earls Path, between the pond and the Robin Hood, towards the New Road, Fairmead, and Buckhurst Hill. *The Graphic*, 6 May 1882

"The lake at Loughton" -- Staples Rd pond. The structure on the hill is a thatched deershelter, or summerhouse, as the Loughton people called them. Another gave its name to Deershelter Plain, by the Wake Arms. *The Graphic*, 6 May 1882

The Recreation Ground, *Illustrated London News*, 6 May 1882. It is not certain which recreation area is depicted – there were several, including the Stubbles in Loughton, where, as here, swingboats and donkey rides were on offer.

Introduction

Both the history of Loughton and its present are inextricably linked to its Forest. 1300 acres of Epping Forest are situated in Loughton, which is more than twice the whole area of Burnham Beeches, and more than a third of the area of the whole parish. Norman Scarfe, in the *Shell Guide to Essex* wrote of Loughton "trees hold their own in this otherwise suburban town". That is a gross understatement: there are, perhaps, ten trees for every Loughtonian. Yet it is surprising how little Loughton folk know and use the Forest, excepting always dog-owners, horse-riders, and toddler-walkers. It is always there, on the western and northern edge of the town, no more than twenty minutes' walk from the furthest corner of Loughton. But on many of these walks, we have quite often seen nobody at all more than fifty yards from the Forest edge.

In local history, it was the opportunity the Forest gave for grazing animals and supplying fuel that gave Loughton the kernel of its economy for perhaps a thousand years, and gave it and the other forest villages something of an edge over purely agricultural places. It was the defence of those rights by one Loughton working man, Thomas Willingale, and the support given him by public-spirited people such as the Buxtons, that led to a stay of execution for Epping Forest when commons all over the country were being enclosed for private profit. And the Corporation of London, who subsequently made Loughton the headquarters of the Forest administration, finally achieved its preservation. For 124 years, they have exercised their benign guardianship of this wonderful asset, and at no expense to the district.

The Forest has never been enclosed and cultivated, but it has been *managed* by man throughout its written history. It is not, and never has been in historic times, an entirely natural landscape, a wildwood, a British jungle, as some commentators have alleged. Since Norman times, it has been a wood pasture; and in the early centuries, a royal forest, where other activity was subordinated to the preservation of game for the royal enjoyment.

A wood-pasture means essentially the maintenance of an area for the twin purposes of providing timber and grazing, and implies a mixture of grassland and wooded areas. The Forest in Loughton was formerly very much more open grass than it is now. As we take the walks in this book, there will be times when we say "the view from this point was formerly open and extensive – now it is closed by tree growth". That is the result of the great decline of grazing over the last 100 years, and of the cessation of pollarding – which was the cutting back of trees to head height on a cycle every few years. As a result of this, the forest canopy has become much more dense, cutting off the light below the trees that enabled the growth of many species, particularly of wild flowers, that the Victorians saw as common, but which are now rare or extinct in our Forest.

Much though we may regret these losses, what an asset Loughtonians have on their doorsteps! The bustle and business of the modern High Road is left behind when you enter the woodland. The air is purer and more exhilarating. The thousands rushing for the train, queuing in the supermarket, hastening to the M25, are far away. Depending on the wind and where in the Forest you are, the sound of traffic may well be in the background. However, you are less than 15 miles from Charing Cross, but you might as well be in the Highlands. The Forest is owned and managed by its conservators – the Corporation of London, but nobody directs you which path you can take, or where you must enter the Forest. You can do so in the heat of summer, when the asphalt on the roads melts, in the snow, in heavy rain, or when a gale whips in a thousand acres of trees a noise louder than an aircraft taking off. In fact, the Forest is often at its most attractive in extreme conditions, and it changes remarkably when night falls. Owls are numerous and vocal, even on the Forest edge, and all sorts of rustlings and strange noises reach your ears; from the haunting call of the vixen, to the strange, staccato, bark of the muntjac.

These are short walks, mostly of about an hour's duration, in that part of Epping Forest situated in the parish of Loughton. They are designed for non-specialist strollers rather than for purposeful and experienced ramblers, to whom we suspect they would seem rather short and tame. The Forest, with its mostly clay soils, can get rather wet. In winter, and after heavy rain in summer, sound, well-fitting footwear is called for. A walking stick is useful for beating down the odd bramble, or to assist anyone a bit unsteady, but not essential. The times we give are those that might be expected for a fairly gentle family stroll, taking time to admire a view, and the occasional rest on a handy log, and the distances include diversions to walk round a pond or to avoid a muddy patch or fallen tree.

These are walks that anyone, a group, or a family, can fit into a Sunday afternoon, or the odd hour at any time of year. They are ideal for Loughtonians who have visitors from afar who want to see the Forest – but remember to tell them to bring stout shoes. We hope they will also be of value to those from farther afield – who may drive out to the numerous pleasant pubs on the forest edge on a summer evening, or stay in our hotel or guest houses, or who visit the 25 or 30 restaurants in and around the High Road. Most of the pubs we mention also serve food.

The Forest is different season by season – the fresh green leaves unfurling in the Spring, the shepherds' crooks of the bracken fronds, the catkins and blossom; welcome shade in high summer, with sun-baked ruts like iron grooves in the path, and the dried up shingle beds of the streams, along which you can often walk. In autumn, of course, the colours are magnificent. They do not approach the vivid tints of the New England fall, but their chrome yellows and browns still give subtle beauty. Later, the forest floor is carpeted with leaves, acorns, and beech-mast, and the winter winds howl through the trees. Once in a while, snow covers all, and transforms the whole scene into a strange and beautiful white sculpture, when families from the town go up to the Forest for sledging or snowball fights.

Whatever the season or the weather, do get out in the Forest. If you live in Loughton, you can do so at a moment's notice. If you come from further afield, then a car or train journey may be called for. Whichever way you come, you will not be disappointed.

The authors are very grateful to Richard Morris, one of the Verderers for the Northern part of the Forest, for reading and commenting on a draft of this booklet. Any errors that remain are, of course, their own. They are grateful to the Field Studies Council for permission to reproduce the maps. The maps, from James Brimble's *London's Epping Forest,* are to be reissued as a separate publication.

Note – car parking is possible in many places provided by the Conservators. Many people, however, find it more secure to leave cars other than in car parks, on street at the forest edge, and that is what for the most part we recommend. Please park considerately, and if you are not from Loughton, note where you have left your car. It isn't much use as with one couple we heard of, merely to remember you parked under a large tree!

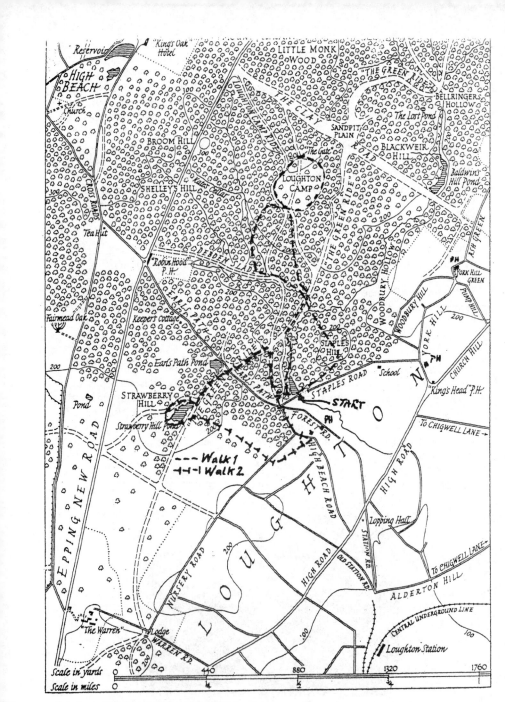

Walks 1 and 2

Walk 1
Loughton Camp

- Start point: Staples Road Pond. Distance: 3.4 miles. Time: 1hour 10 minutes approx. Terrain: hilly, wet in winter. The land rises from about 140ft at the beginning to 300ft at Loughton Camp. Refreshments: two pubs (the Royal Oak and Victoria, Forest Rd) about 100yards into Loughton from the start /finish point. Car parking: on street in Shaftesbury by the dam (avoid school collection/delivery times).

  - If you get lost anywhere on the first three walks, remember all the streams drain down to Staples Road Pond.

From the centre of the dam over Staples Road Pond, take the steps on your left down to the dipping platform, and then walk along the red path behind the wooden post and rail fence.

Staples Road Pond, also called the Reservoir, was dug about 1880 as a flood precaution. It was full by 1882, when some builders working on constructing Glendower and Forest Villa rescued a woman who had fallen into the pond. The Loughton Brook has always been prone to flood the centre of Loughton, because of the probability, about every 5 years, of abnormally heavy rain on the forest ridge causing the lower reaches of the Brook, after it leaves the Forest, to overflow. The Reservoir was never a source of drinking water, but before piped water was laid on, people used it to collect water for washing.

In the 1960-1990 period, the pond became badly silted up so as almost to disappear, and the estate of houses called Shaftesbury was built lower down across the course of the brook. In 1982, serious floods in the Staples Rd/ Shaftesbury area ensued. In 1995, the pond was deepened, and the present dam built, designed to withstand the worst surge of water calculated to be expected in a 75-year period. The banks around the dam are flower-rich – when it had been completed, the grassland was sown with the seed of typical wild plants from the area.

Follow the brook/pond inlet on its western side, crossing it by a wooden railed bridge. Cross a second bridge, this time without rails, and leave the path, climbing the valley side on the west, until you come to the Green Ride, a wide path for walkers and riders, turning right on to it.

The Green Ride was cut through the Forest in preparation for its official dedication by Queen Victoria in 1882. She was driven along it in an open carriage to High Beech. (or Beach; nobody is sure which spelling to use.) It is a well-known walk in its own right, but in these walks we follow only short stretches of it. This part of the Green Ride was an open trackway before the Ride proper was constructed. It was known as the Ridings, and may have been a dividing line in the woodland.

Follow the ride down the slope to where it crosses a tributary of the Loughton Brook by a culvert. Turn sharp left once over the stream onto a path going westwards. This section can be boggy. You can avoid it by going through the trees to its north.

After about 50 yards, the path divides. Take the right fork, going uphill. This path dives below beech and hornbeam, with prominent roots across the path (take care!) and in wet weather becomes a runnel off the hillside. As you climb the hill, notice how large and stately beeches take over, in a more open landscape. Towards the top of the hill, notice the many-stemmed beeches, with grotesque gnarled shapes. This is the result first of coppicing, which was the cutting off of the tree at ground level, leaving it to regenerate in as many as half a dozen stems round the old stump. After this, the individual stems – which had become in time trunks in their own right, were subjected in this part of Loughton to lopping, whereby the trees were "topped" at shoulder height, allowing many branches to spring from the cut, which were later lopped for firewood.

The last lopping was in 1879, and thereafter, the trees grew into strange and deformed shapes. Lopping was practised over much of Loughton, except in Monk Wood and Loughton Piece, but coppicing was common only several hundred years ago, and in this area of Loughton Camp. The coppiced, then pollarded, beeches have been living for perhaps as much as 700 years, making them the oldest living things in the area. After the cessation of lopping, the canopy of the forest also became much denser, preventing much of the growth of flowers and other plants, for which this area was noted, on the floor of the wood.

After a few silver birches, you will see the ramparts of Loughton Camp up ahead. They take the form of a ditch and bank, in roughly circular form. Go up onto the mound, and bear left, proceeding clockwise around the bank, taking note of landmarks such as notice boards - it is easy to become disoriented on the camp, especially when there is no sun. Note the contorted, many-trunked beeches, in which children love to play hide and seek. Squirrel, rabbit and woodpecker are often found on the camp. In the snow, you will often see tracks of fox, fallow, and muntjac. It had the last active badger sett in the Forest, disused by 1961.

Loughton Camp is a scheduled ancient monument, but has never been thoroughly excavated or investigated. It is a roughly circular defensive hill-fort, dating to the Iron Age. The banks have become eroded over the centuries, and may well have been topped by a defensive fence or palisade. The total area is about 11 acres.

In the Forest also is a similar, but larger encampment at Ambresbury, about half a mile north of the Wake Arms roundabout; there is no truth in the commonly told story that the two camps saw Boadicea's last stand against the Romans. The camps have to be envisaged in a landscape much more thinly wooded than at present, where sighting of an enemy would be easy. Nowadays they would make poor defensive positions.

The views from Loughton Camp were once superb, extending to the south over London. But these gradually got hemmed in by tree growth, and are now non-existent. (see map) The camp was the setting for the supposed murder in R Austin Freeman's detective story *The Jacob Street Mystery* (1942). The participants come down by train from Fenchurch Street to Loughton Station, and take exactly the way described in this walk to the Camp.

The Camp was not recognised as an ancient monument before about 1880. d'Oyley, the Loughton surveyor, who drew up the maps for the Epping Forest Commission, marks only the area to its north, as Dick Turpin's Cave; which appellation later got applied to a pub in High Beech. Turpin was indeed active in the Forest in highway robbery and burglary. Old houses in Loughton had their upper storeys closed off at night by a flap and prop called the Turpin Trap, but most of the stories told about him are apocryphal.

Follow the bank round (at one point it seems to peter out into a bog, but in fact carries on the other side) until you get to the point at which you entered. Then descend into the ditch, or fosse, below the bank, and carry on until you come to a path on the left after about 100 yards. The path is on the steepest part of the ramparts, which can be better appreciated here than from the mound. The path starts where there is a clump of five beeches, formed from an old coppice stool, on your left. Descend by the path, down the hillside, until you come to a plank bridge, which crosses the officially unnamed tributary of the Loughton Brook sometimes called the Debden Slade Brook. This area is called Kate's Cellar. Cross this bridge onto the south side of the brook, and follow this bank, with its mossy sides, through pollard beeches and hornbeam. Several uprooted trees at this point have fallen towards the stream: note their small rootballs. You then come on your right to another bridge: cross it to the north side (the ground on the north side gets boggy, usually because of mountain bike use) and go through a thicket of holly, until in about 50 yards you come to the open clearing, Debden Slade. The vegetation here is mostly bracken, bramble and oak seedlings and saplings, no longer kept at bay by the commoners' cattle, for which the Slade was a favourite grazing place. A fine crab apple is situated on the right hand side of the Slade, halfway along.

The Slade was formerly much bigger than at present, and was the place to which the poor children entertained at the Shaftesbury Retreat (see the LDHS

-8-

publication, *From Mean Streets to Epping Forest*) played games. Continue following the stream on its north bank, until you come back to the culvert on the Green Ride. Cross the culvert, and follow the stream on its south side until it rejoins the main Loughton Brook. Cross the brook by the earthen bridge, and carry straight on up the hill.

This conical hill is Staples Hill and is mainly hornbeam, beech and holly. 'Staple' is the Old English *stapol*, meaning marker-post, and this may have some relevance to marking or pointing the way to Loughton Camp, on the adjacent hill.

At the top, by some fallen trees, you will see the outline of James Cubitt's Staples Road Schools ahead and to the left. The views from Staples Hill are not as good as they once were, because of tree growth, but in winter, you can still see across to Shooters Hill in South London.

It was on Staples Hill that the inhabitants of Loughton used to gather at midnight on 11 November (or 1 November until 1752) in each year ceremonially to inaugurate the lopping season. With much carousing, the first blow was struck, and the first bough severed, and some of the loppers believed that if the custom was not observed, then the lopping rights would be voided. The last lopping was on 11 November 1879, after a night of drinking at, and a torchlit procession from, the Crown Inn. Lopping continued latterly until 23 April in the following year.

Bear diagonally right across the grassy area and pass a large standing stump 8ft high to your left. The path descends with more views to emerge opposite Forest Villa and the Retreat House (Melbourn Cottage) in Staples Rd, adjacent to the dam. For information on the houses and school in Staples Rd, see the LDHS publication, *A Walk round Loughton*. In winter, the air around Staples Road is often still laden with wood smoke, as many of the households seem still to like to burn logs.

Nowadays, however, the old Loughton custom of *wooding* – that is, going into the Forest to collect driftwood – is almost forgotten, though still permitted within certain limits. (You can collect no more than 28lbs of wood per day. Each piece may be no more than six inches in circumference and 3ft in length) What of course was *not* allowed was the assisting of living wood to *become* driftwood, which was usually accomplished by a strong line with a weight attached, which would be looped round a frail-looking branch and pulled down.

Staples Hill holds a large population of grey squirrels. They are of course found everywhere in the Forest – the last reds died out about 1960. Attempts were made by the Forest authorities to exterminate the greys, but this was given up as hopeless in about 1965. The Staples Hill squirrels not only feed on woodland products, especially beechmast and hornbeam seeds, but also cross the road to raid dustbins, gardens, and even kitchens. In this way, they extend their food supply and active season, and thus their numbers, and can often be seen re-crossing the road with a crust of bread or biscuit in their jaws. The Staples Hill squirrels are also very vocal. Fred Speakman, the High Beech naturalist, wrote of squirrels emitting tiny sounds, inaudible within a few feet, but the population on Staples Hill, possibly because of its density, can often be heard churring and chirruping at full volume.

Road or the path inside the forest edge will lead you back to the start of the walk.

Overlooking Debden Slade, 1886

Loughton Camp, *The Graphic*, 6 May 1882.

Tree cover in the Loughton Camp area, 1890s and 1983. *Field Studies*, 6 (1985) p. 287. These are from an article on Forest management by R L Layton. Reproduced by kind permission of the Field Studies Council.

1890

A104

ROBIN HOOD (PH)

EARLS PATH

GREEN RIDE

DEBDEN SLADE

LOUGHTON CAMP

CLAY ROAD

1983

A104

ROBIN HOOD (PH)

EARLS PATH

GREEN RIDE

DEBDEN SLADE

LOUGHTON CAMP

CLAY ROAD

SCALE

0   200   400   600   800   1000   METRES

 WOODLAND

 WOODLAND / HEATHLAND

GRASSLAND / HEATHLAND

- - - ROADS

Walk 2
Three Ponds

- Start point: Staples Road Pond. Distance: 2 miles. Time, 50 min. approx. Terrain: mostly level or with gentle rises, ground more firm than on many Forest walks. Refreshments: as walk 1.

From the middle of the Staples Road dam (walk 1) follow the path along the bank left. For details of the Reservoir, or Staples Road Pond, see walk 1. Walk between two metal posts, and go straight ahead between the trees, until you come out very shortly on to a wide, unsurfaced, path.

Turn right on to this path, and continue gently uphill, between beeches and holly, until you come to the wide, gravelled, Green Ride. Turn left on to the Ride, walking between stands of beech and oak, many of which post-date the lopping era, and are therefore spear trees. In about 10 minutes from the start, you reach the Earls Path car park, either side of the Loughton - High Beech road. Take care in crossing the road: there is a 60 mph speed limit at this point, and cars tend to speed down the hill.

This area, to the north of Earl's Path, was one of those cleared and parcelled out into ¼ acre building plots in the 1860s. Fortunately, no actual building took place, and with the passing of the Epping Forest Act of 1878, and the subsequent arbitration by Sir Arthur Hobhouse, all these plots were returned to the Forest.

Earls Path Pond is on the south side of the road. Like all the ponds in the Forest, it is man-made, but whereas Staples Road Pond was dug for flood control, that at Earls Path was excavated for gravel extraction, and was formed about 1890. Each parish had to maintain its own roads, and good sources of road metal in the form of gravel were very much sought after. The parish sometimes gave work to unemployed labourers in digging out and carting the gravel, and Earls Path, where the pit was adjacent to a road, must have been convenient for this purpose.

The pits, when flooded, became pleasant ponds, and Earls Path, with its white water lilies, spatterdocks, irises, rushes, and water mint, is an especially pleasant roadside lake, very popular with fishermen. Presumably at some time the pond was deliberately stocked, as it is not fed by any brook or stream. Earls Path Pond is also rich in amphibians, and the area between here and Staples Road is one of the places in the Forest where lizards are seen. Along Earls Path, between here and the Robin Hood pub, are numerous other gravel diggings and holes, on both sides of the road, which fill up with water in times of heavy rain, forming a strange, semi-aquatic landscape.

Follow the gravelled ride along the east side of the pond, and after about 220 yards, bear left, when the water of Strawberry Hill Pond comes in sight.

Strawberry Hill lies to the south of Earls Path and the east of the Epping New Road, which was built in 1830 alongside the western boundary of Loughton, one of the first by-passes in the country. The pond, along with Earls Path and other ponds further to the north, resulted from gravel digging for this and other roads.

Strawberry Hill Pond is completely different from those at Earls Path and Staples Road. Its banks are bare, showing at all times of year the reddish gravel and shingly soil. Old Loughton folk call it "the Gravels" for this reason. The roots of trees stick out from the banks, often in crazy contortions. This undermining of trees, leaving the roots exposed, was common in gravel extraction, when it was forbidden actually to uproot or destroy any tree in the operations. A number of the trees, destabilised by the banks, lean at strange angles, or have become dwarfed.

Strawberry Hill Pond is very much a place for children, who love to run and hide among the banks, feed the ducks, and climb on the trees, some of which are particularly well adapted for that purpose, provided parents exercise due caution. There is an island, on which the wildfowl can take refuge, and much bracken and gorse, the latter often in flower even in winter (the old country saying goes, *when gorse's out of flower, kissing's out of fashion*).

Trees round the pond include beech and oak (with one strange clump of trees on the north-west side seeming to be three oaks and two beeches all out of the same stump, with a holly thrown in for good measure) and also, on the west side, sweet chestnut, which bear their small nuts cocooned in many and long – spined seed cases in autumn. A single old crab on the west side is laden with fruit in the autumn. The open area to the west of the pond is one of the parts of the forest where flowers are common; purple heather, foxglove, and coltsfoot, for instance. Rabbits inhabit the heath, and keep the grass well-cropped.

Walk all round the pond until you can see the surfaced ride ahead. Cross it by a many-trunked beech, and walk straight ahead, with two recently repollarded beeches on the right of the path, for about 200 yards, when a plain unfolds ahead. This area, the Stubbles, was also enclosed for eventual building. On the right hand side beyond a hedge is Fairhead's Nursery, formerly Paul's, from which the public cannot be excluded, but which is not generally traversed.

Winter in Epping Forest, *Pictorial World*, 22 January 1876. Gathering of ice, and of fresh water from under it, before refrigeration and piped water supply, was common in the Forest in the nineteenth century.

This plain, also home to numerous rabbits, has a number of seedling and sapling oaks growing in the grass, and at its centre, a fine clump of six beeches and an oak. Walk along the plain till you get to the Nursery Road car park. Turn left into the road, and carry on downhill till a small plain opens up on the right. Nursery Road was one of the streets laid out by Maitland – see below, Walk 3.

One of the best panoramas of the town is visible from the seat on this clearing. On the right is the grey tower and flagpole of St John's Church, which replaced Loughton's mediaeval church in 1844, with some fine cedars in front; and rising in the centre is Queens Road, with the houses of Pump Hill at its summit. To the left are the Staples Road schools.

Walk along the path by the seat. As you near the belt of trees, the backs of the houses in Staples Road, ended by the green tower of Forest Villa, come into sight. Many of the houses in Staples Road, two storeys from the front, are three or four at the back, because of their hillside sites. Enter the wood and carry on obliquely left, with the gardens of Forest View Road on your right. The path emerges at the junction of that road and Smarts Lane, with the two pubs, the Victoria Tavern and the Royal Oak. On the opposite corner was Ney's Retreat, or the Cyclists' Rest cafe, now a private house. Turn left into Smarts Lane, with additional views between the houses, and walk along it between two necks of the Forest. That on the left was formerly a clearing where swings and amusements were offered.

Cross Earls Path into Shaftesbury (formerly Staples Road; renamed 1996) and return to your starting point.

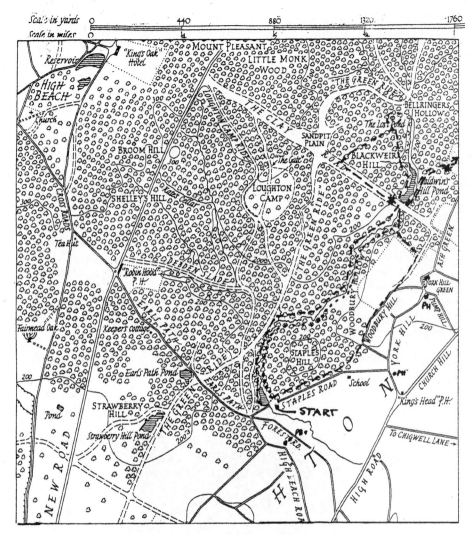

Walk 3 ------   Alternative ·········

Walk 3

The Loughton Brook and Blackweir Hill Pond

- Start point: Staples Road Pond. Distance: 3.5 miles, 1½ hours approx. The walk can be shortened to the round hour by omitting the Blackweir Hill Pond. Terrain: level, then with distinct and gentle rises, ground; wet near brook after rain, otherwise quite dry, especially on Blackweir Hill. Refreshments: as walk 1, plus the Foresters' Arms, at Baldwin's Hill, and the Gardeners' Arms at York Hill Green.

As in walk 1, from the centre of the dam over Staples Road Pond, take the steps on your left down to the dipping platform, and then walk along the red path behind the wooden post and rail fence. Cross the railed and plank footbridges, but keep to the western bank of the Loughton Brook – do not climb the bank to the Green Ride as in walk 1.

The Loughton Brook takes the water falling on a very wide sector of the Forest stretching approximately from the Loughton parish boundary on the west as far north as the Wake Arms and as far east as the A121. West of this watershed, the streams drain into the Lea, but the Brook is a tributary of the Roding, which it joins nowadays at the end of Roding Road, pursuing a sinuous course between the Drive and Forest Road, then behind Brooklyn Avenue and through the grounds of the Roding Valley High School. It is a noted geomorphologic feature, a river in "old age" that has carved out a deep valley in the gravels and clays of the hill caps. Easily noted is the undercutting of one side of the banks, and deposition on the other, with many sinuous bends. The bed of the brook is pebble gravel.

Cross the side stream that leads in from Debden Slade, bearing right back to the main brook, and then turn left, alongside the brook. The path can get muddy in the winter, but you can walk equally well a few yards higher up the valley side. The brookside path is a favourite haunt of snakes. Should you see one, do not be afraid. Most are grass snakes, which are quite harmless, and the occasional adder will be shy and will not harm you unless attacked.

Follow the path on the west side, passing a bridge over the stream, at the top of the clearing, beyond which you can see the white-painted Loughton Lodge.

The whole area of the brook was cleared in 1997, but there has been considerable regrowth of shrubs and saplings since. As you carry on northward, there are some good recently pollarded oaks. The valley becomes a bit barer and more open, and you cross another side stream coming in from the west (no bridge but only a long pace or short jump). The trees are now predominantly beech. Pick your way over the roots of a nice 2-stemmed beech, up the grassed bank of the dam over Baldwins Hill Pond.

Baldwins Hill Pond was dug at the same time as that at Staples Road. It lies higher, and the dam is crossed by a broad ride called the Clay Road. This was another of the roads laid out, but in this case not metalled, by J W Maitland when he, as Lord of the Manor, tried in 1864 to enclose all of Loughton's forest. Had it been developed, the heart would have been torn out of the woodland. The Pond was cleared, and the outlet rebuilt, in 2000. It is a pleasant small lake, with a clearing beyond.

On to Lost Pond (you can return to the start at this point by crossing the dam and recommencing the walk at *)

Turn left along the Clay Road (or Clay Ride or Path as it is sometimes called). The western part of this road is much more overgrown than the eastern, with a pleasing mixture of sedge, dog rose, gorse, bramble, and bracken. The trees are oak, beech and hornbeam, with many saplings. No doubt the conservators will eventually clear the area. Note the channel made by an occasional stream through the gravel, as water forms runnels off the hillside.

Just before you reach the clearing (Sandpit Plain) at the top, where the Green Ride crosses the Clay Path, you will see a path on your right, entering the trees in a direction of about 4 o'clock. The path is well marked at first, but especially in autumn, becomes obscured by leaves. Keep along the path, bearing generally left (if you bear right you will come back to the Clay Path). After a few minutes, you will see the Lost Pond in its slight dip.

The Lost Pond, or Blackweir Hill Pond, is often reckoned the most picturesque of all Forest ponds. It is entirely girt about by trees, mostly beeches, with some silver birch. On summer days, the light is superb, dappled by the leaves, and in winter, the stark beauty of the trunks, thrown into relief by rime, stands out against the half-frozen water.

Make a circuit anti-clockwise of the pond, noting an 11-stemmed beech, which must have sprung from an ancient stool in the last 150 or so years. It is at this point you will leave the pond when you have made a circuit of it. On the east side of the pond stood until recently the climbing tree – a hornbeam into whose straight trunk had been screwed iron rungs, said to have been a Home Guard exercise, which children could climb. This tree fell in the 1990s, and has not been replaced.

Another practice frowned on by the Conservators, of course, is carving on trees. It is especially prevalent here, where large, smooth-trunked beeches abound. None of the hundreds of inscriptions still visible are very old – the trees seem to bleed them out after about 30 years. One wonders, however, whether the Barbara who loves me of 1965 still does, and whether JJA and RR from 1970 are still together!

When you have completed the walk round the pond, set off downhill and generally right from the 11-trunked beech. At the foot of the dip is a small stream, which you can cross by a beech that is strangely broken off about 4ft from the ground. In a minute or so, you come out to the top of Baldwin's Hill Pond. Follow its western side till you get back to the Clay Path.

*If you have omitted Blackweir Hill, this is where you rejoin the walk.

Cross the dam, and carry on along the eastern side of the pond. The path leads into a clearing, and a long and quite steep hillside, at the top of which the Foresters' Arms pub can be seen. This hillside was thinned in 2001, and once again, the pond is visible from the road as it was in the nineteenth century. The trees that remain, oak and hornbeam, have grown since the cessation of lopping in 1879, and are quite sizeable. The banks of grass at Woodbury Hill and Baldwins Hill still maintain more flower species than much of the forest, including heather, scabious, wood-anemone and cow-wheat.

You can either return along the west bank of the brook, or by a mixture of path and forest edge higher up. The brookside walk has already been described, but the variation is as follows.

Keep to the mid-point of the hill until a paling fence comes into view. This is the northern boundary of land belonging to Dryad's Hall, which was enclosed by Robin Allen for his house, then called Woodberry, in the mid-nineteenth century.

Robin Allen was secretary of Trinity House in London, and one of Loughton's first commuters, as he declared in his memorandum to the Epping Forest Commissioners in July 1876. The enclosure he made, much of which is wooded in an indistinguishable way from the surrounding Forest, was allowed to remain by the 1880 Arbitration.

Follow this fence on its north-eastern face about 20 yards from it (it gets wet nearer the fence) until you come out onto a track leading to Dryad's Hall itself, which you pass on your right. After the death of Allen, the Hall was the home (called "Mansfield") first of Percy Alden, the radical journalist, social researcher, and MP for Tottenham, and then, renamed in the 1920s, of Oswald Silberrad, who had invented the means of detonating TNT. Follow the track right until you come to a triangle and the street, Woodbury Hill. At a house just to the left is a blue plaque to Sarah Flower and William Bridges Adams, respectively hymnodist and poet, and railway engineer, inventor, and pamphleteer. For further details of this area, and of Staples Rd, see *Walk Round Loughton*.

However, you need to turn right. Take the path down the side of Woodbury Knoll, a house built by G L Bruce in 1903. This is said to incorporate its predecessor buildings, Lincoln's Cottages, within the fabric. The path leads up to Woodbury Hollow, or the Hole, where a pair of 17-18th century cottages remain, plus a house designed by M H Baillie Scott for the Zimmermann family, whose initials remain in the gable end. Rejoin Woodbury Hill by turning right, and carry on past Loughton Lodge into the Forest. From the large chestnut tree (seat) outside Loughton Lodge is an excellent open view across to the terrain covered by walk 2 and to High Beech – even in summer you can see the spire of its church. Beyond the two rustic posts across the track, at the top of Forest Way, 100 yards further on, take the path down the hill through the wood, rather than turning left down the road. This takes you down the north side of Staples Hill and out to what remains of Harding's Plain, outside Staples Road School. In safer times, till about 1970, this grassed area was used by the schoolchildren as their playground. Turn right just inside the forest edge on to the path that skirts Staples Road, or walk along the road itself, back to the starting point (300 yards).

Cottage near York Hill. This is thought to be near Woodbury Hollow.

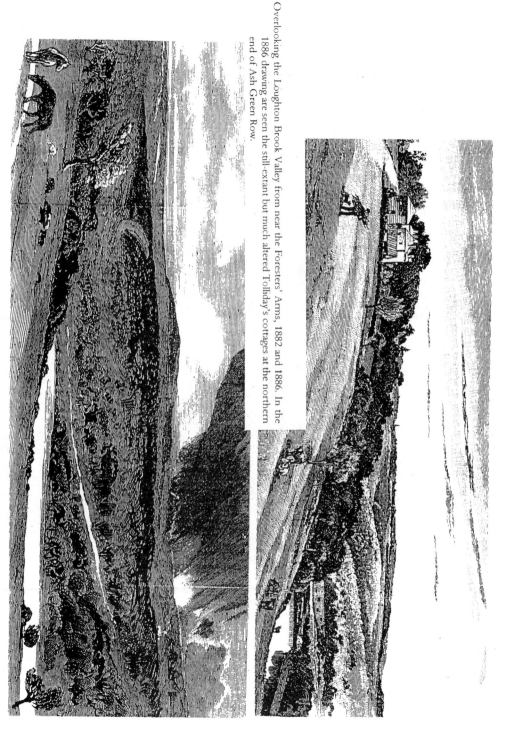

Overlooking the Loughton Brook Valley from near the Foresters' Arms, 1882 and 1886. In the 1886 drawing are seen the still-extant but much altered Tolliday's cottages at the northern end of Ash Green Row.

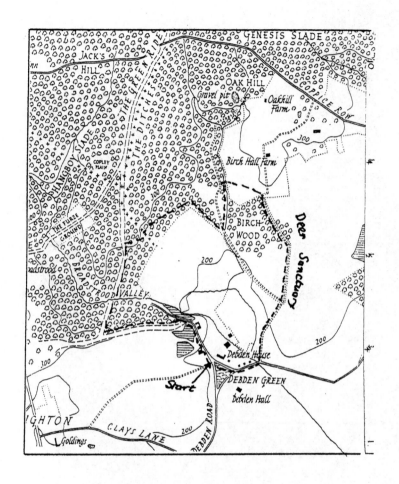

Walk 4

Walk 4

Debden Green, the Deer Sanctuary, and Loughton (or Debden) Parks

- Start point: Debden Green. Distance: 3.1 miles. Time: 1 hour 10 min. Terrain – hilly, the beginning of the walk muddy in winter or after rain. The land rises from 185ft at the beginning to about 340ft at the summit, half-way. Refreshments; none (there is a café, the Nosebag, in the old stables of Debden House, open during the camping season, April-Oct; but this is intended for campsite users). In August and September, this is a good walk for blackberrying. Bus: 20, 167, 804, H1 to corner Pyrles Lane/Chester Road, and walk (1/2 mile). Car parking: on street by Debden House, at Ripley View, or on small triangle of land at the start of the walk – do not obstruct entries. Do not park in Debden Lane itself.

- If you get lost on this walk, all the streams drain down to the campsite.

This walk starts from the signposted public footpath in Debden Lane, adjacent to the three cottages on the left hand side. This was an old green lane, now encroached on by sapling growth, shown on the Chapman and Andre map of 1777. The three houses, Debden Villas, at one time called Alpha, Beta, and Gamma, were built about 100 years ago by W R Clarke of Debden Hall (which was on the site of Ripley View and is now demolished). Follow the path uphill, with the paling fence on your right. It can become very muddy after rain, but there are numerous tracks off to the left, which skirt the worst areas. On your left are the grounds of Debden House, which is owned by Newham Borough Council and is used as an educational centre and campsite - in the summer you will see the tents and vans of the campers.

There is a good deal of vegetation along the path by no means common throughout the forest; for example, field maple, elm, hawthorn, and further up, wild service. There are also many blackberries – in the autumn this whole walk is well provided with them – and many suckers of English elm. Dutch Elm disease affected this corner of Essex badly from the 1960s, and many tall elms had to be felled. The stools sucker freely, but when the young growth gets to a certain size, it too succumbs. If the main path is very muddy, it is worth cutting diagonally right across the field beyond the campsite, where there is often a mowed swathe, and entering the wood at the top, turning right along the path just inside the woodland to rejoin the main path higher up where it is drier.

After about 10 minutes, you are in Birch Wood, a later addition to the Forest, once zoned by Loughton Urban District Council for housing. The high wire fence of the Epping Forest Deer Sanctuary comes in sight on the right. The Sanctuary, 108 acres in extent, was purchased by the Conservators and instituted in 1960. It is not part of the legal Forest. The deer could at one time use leaps to get into the Forest proper, but these have now been closed, and the Forest and Sanctuary deer do not mix.

Some fine oaks and beeches dot the wood and surrounding land from here. Birch Wood was an area of coppice, though coppicing must have ceased a long time ago. Do not try to cross the patch of bramble or scrub you see at first – this will just frighten any deer that happen to be nearby. Wait until you get to a point where the fence is only a couple of yards from the path. It is often possible to see lone deer, or groups, especially with binoculars, in the deer park in front of you, with the green bulk of Gaunt's and Ruddock's (or Redoaks) Woods (Theydon Bois) in the distance. There are also distant views across Essex towards Ongar. As you near the fence, you cross the parish boundary (unmarked) between Theydon Bois and Loughton. Follow the path parallel to the fence (it goes through several dead and dying beeches at this point) onwards to the back entrance of the deer sanctuary, where the (very strict) regulations concerning it are posted. In particular, there is never any public access to the Sanctuary.

This point is another good place from which to observe the deer. The building up ahead is Birch Hall Farm; Birch Hall (Theydon Bois) itself is beyond. Birch Hall and Wood are curious misnomers, since there are few birches in this wood where beech is most noticeable. In old records, the spelling is "Burch", and this may indicate a derivation from the old *buch*, which became in modern English *beech*.

A stile in the fence on your left leads to a path diagonally set across a meadow, part of the Forest buffer-land. In the far corner, though obscured by bushes, are another stile and a rather rickety bridge over the stream. Ignore the bridge on the right-hand side of the field: this just leads into the adjacent meadow. Cross the bridge, re-enter the Forest, and follow the stream on its far (west) bank in a left hand (with the flow) direction. This is a very fine valley, with many beeches. The stream enters a culvert, and the Debden House campsite is again visible ahead.

Debden House owned the fields hereabouts, which William Waller described accurately as "park-like"; they were indeed called "Loughton Parks". Many rabbits graze on the slopes here, and venture onto the Forest as well. Hares are not unknown. There are good, and unusual, views of the Forest, which surrounds on all sides the fields of the Parks.

Turn right onto the path just inside the Forest. At the first turn in the boundary, you come to a cleared area, where there are some convenient logs for resting.

Fallen trees are valuable to the Forest ecology as a habitat for insects and other invertebrates, and are also home to many fungi. These are especially noticeable in the autumn, and include bracket fungus, and (usually earlier) oyster mushroom. On the forest floor are to be found many others, including shaggy inkcap, and fly agaric. There also seem to be more than the usual number of birds hereabouts, including tits, nuthatches, robins, and wrens.

Take the lower of the two paths (the one nearer the campsite), which enters an area with a group of seven pollard beeches, and numerous fallen trees. Ahead is one of the largest beeches in this part of the Forest, a huge specimen with a massive canopy, and a many stemmed trunk six or seven paces round the base. It was no doubt a coppice stool that sent up several trunks that over the centuries knitted together. Keep well to the left of this tree, the path going through an area of bracken and birch. Keeping left, follow the path along the ridge – dotted with large beeches – and pass on your immediate left a curious straight line of five beeches and an oak. It was in this area that deep ditches were cut as tank traps in 1940; they were later filled in. This is a good area in which to see the forest deer.

You will see the surfaced line of the Green Ride ahead of you; turn left onto it, until you cross the Broadstrood stream by a bridge. Just beyond the bridge, turn left on to another ride. This descends with a couple of turns, including one over a wide railed bridge over another stream. Hedgerow shrubs, including elder, sloe, and many blackberries flank the ride.

After a few minutes, you come to the forest gate. From the path that goes off to the right just before it, you can see the back of Hartshill (now Forest Rise), a grand house built by Edmond Egan for John Gregson.

Go through the gate. On your left are the buildings of a former farm, and then the white painted Debden Mount, once in the possession of the Upton and Warwick families, a handsome house of mid-19th century appearance, and on the right, Elm Cottage, once the home of the van der Gucht family, probably of 17th century origin, a "lobby-entrance" house. After some newer houses comes early-19th century Debden House itself, home of the Standidge and Pryor families: it was bought by the East Ham County Borough Council in 1949, and is kept by their successors in first-class order, with pleasant gardens. Day-camping facilities are available for a nominal charge, whereby you can roam through the grounds, have a picnic or barbecue, and see this walk from the "inside" of the park.

It is also worth walking along the north-east side of the green to look at Algars, formerly The Beeches, another of Loughton's weatherboarded houses, again of 17th century origin. On the other side of the main lane, further south, are the forlorn entrance gates, some 200 years old, of the former Debden Hall. The wooded land hereabouts, though in the Green Belt, is the former garden of Debden Hall—as late as 1955 it was not wooded, and is not part of the Forest – it is in the hands of a land company. In this old garden, on the Grosvenor Rise side, is a strange mound, marked as an antiquity, but which has not been excavated. Here also is Home Mead, which is being preserved as a nature reserve by Epping Forest Council.

Further along Debden Lane towards Theydon Bois, the last house in Loughton, is the superb mock-Tudor country house, Ripley Grange (no admittance, and not visible from the road). It was built in the 1930s by Charles Clarke, owner of the Caribonum Company, has 40 acres of garden, and was on sale in 1999 for £4million.

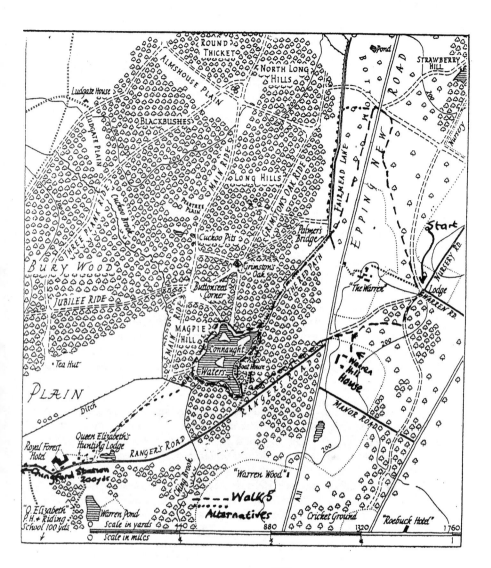

Walk 5

Note: Fences were erected in Spring 2002 to the west of the Epping New Road. These are designed to stop the cattle reintroduced to the Forest from straying onto the road. They are not intended to keep the public out – just duck under the rail or use the gates provided.

Walk 5

Fairmead and Connaught Water

- Start point: Entrance to the Warren, Warren Hill. Distance: 3.8 miles. Time: 1hour 20 min. Terrain – Level. Parts of the walk are muddy in winter or after rain, but alternatives are available. Refreshments; none (there is usually an ice-cream van at the Connaught Water car park in summer, but the café there has been closed.) Buses – routes 20, 397, and 549 stop (ask for Spring Grove) by the Horse Pond at the bottom of Warren Hill, the ¼ mile walk. Car parking: on street in Warren Hill or Nursery Road – do not obstruct entries, and do not park at the right angled bend between the two roads.

If you ask any visitor to Epping Forest where Connaught Water is, he or she will reply, "Chingford". But in fact, this, the biggest Forest lake, is not in Chingford at all, but is equally shared between Waltham Abbey and Loughton parishes. The usual approach to it is from Chingford, hence the confusion, but this walk takes in a portion of Loughton's southern boundary that is seldom approached from the town itself.

At the 90-degree bend that forms the junction between Nursery Road and Warren Hill is a gated road that leads to the Warren, home of the Forest administration (generally no admittance). Take the surfaced ride that strikes off between this gated road and Nursery Road – that is, to the north of the keepers' cottages. The path leads between hedgebanks of oak (including at least one exotic Turkey oak) and bramble. After a short distance, it divides. Take the left fork (the right leads to Strawberry Hill Pond; walk 2) and carry on along the surfaced ride. There is a small clearing on the right, with good oaks and silver birch. On your left, you will see the fence of the Warren grounds, and in a field just beyond the fence, a stone obelisk that a former tenant erected to his favourite horse. The obelisk came from Wanstead House when that was demolished. The Warren, formerly an inn, and its grounds, were remodelled as a private residence and garden by Humphry Repton. The traffic of the A104 (ex A11) Epping New Road will be seen beyond.

The path emerges at a gate into the Lincoln's Lane car park. Keep on the south side of the car park, and cross the A104. Take great care, as traffic commonly reaches 70 mph on this straight stretch of road. Note that from about this point, all the streams drain via Connaught Water into the River Ching, and thence into the Lea, whereas before it, they drain into the Loughton Brook and then the Roding.

On the other side of the A104, turn sharp left along an unsurfaced ride almost parallel with the road. However, this ride is frequently very wet, and an alternative route is to carry straight on from where you crossed, until you reach the old Fairmead Bottom Road, now a dead end, onto which you turn left. The ride keeps just to the Loughton side of the (unmarked) boundary with Waltham Holy Cross parish. This road predates the Epping New Road, and was formerly a through route (the Stump Road) from Buckhurst Hill.

Fairmead Bottom, or Loughton Fairmead, was a plain created for hunting purposes. The deer would be driven out of cover of the trees on to the plain, where a grandstand (later the Little Standing) was erected in the 16th century for the nobles to watch the chase. The timber frame of the standing remains, incorporated in Warren House.

Path and road will lead you to Palmer's Bridge, about 30 yards from what was the junction with the Epping New Road. The Fairmead Bottom Road was closed to traffic in about 1972, and its surface is now very poor indeed, but it can still be entered by motor vehicles from its junction near the motorcycle meet tea hut at High Beech.

Where the ride joins the road, walk along the road, and take the second path (called the Red Path) on the right, keeping the stream on your right. (The first path, with the stream on the left, leads to Grimston's Oak). For much of its length, the Red Path is the boundary between the two parishes. But note that on the Loughton side, very few of the trees have ever been lopped, despite lopping rights having subsisted till 1879. This area was simply too far from the settlement of Loughton to make lopping viable. Oak predominates in this area, and is especially noticeable in the late autumn, when the oaks generally retain a mantle of yellow leaves after the other trees have shed theirs.

After a few minutes, Connaught Water comes in sight on your right. You may also hear the buzz of model aeroplanes, which are flown on Chingford Plain, about 200 yards south-west. The water is a fine lake, again created in the 1880s, with four islands, three of which are in Loughton, as the parish boundary with Waltham bisects the lake For decades it was one of the prime centres for boating in the Forest, an attraction in its own right. In the 1880s, a paddle steamer plied on the lake, but after that, rowing boats and canoes held their own, until the hirer ceased business in the early 1990s.

Nowadays, the birds reign supreme, and are noted for their variety and interest. Moorhen, coots, mallard, mandarin, great crested grebe, Canada geese, pochard and wigeon are among the waterfowl seen, plus, of course, the mallard. Connaught Water is a favourite place for children to feed the waterfowl, and in winter, the residents are joined by numerous gulls, whose swoopings and altercations cause much merriment. The lake is well stocked with fish, and frequented by anglers. In the spring, during spawning, if you are lucky, you may see the fish leaping from the surface.

Walk round the lake anti-clockwise. The first seat and island you come to are in Loughton, the second, in Waltham; and then on, the western bank is in the latter parish. The edges of the lake have been stabilised of late, and a firm walk the whole way is assured whatever the rainfall, the streamlets that used to cause boggy areas having been carried under the path in pipes. The edges are reasonably clear, allowing appreciation of the fine trees, mostly oak, and the views.

On the southern edge, you come to a brick culvert, which carries the River Ching away to the south, and at that point re-enter Loughton. The culvert replaces a rustic bridge erected when the lake was dug: it is less picturesque, but more efficient. The large car park then comes in sight – carry on round the eastern side of the lake, past the site of the old boathouse and tea hut, back to where you joined it. Turn right onto the Red Path, back to the car park, and then walk left along Rangers Road to its junction with the Epping New Road. (You can also go on to Chingford by turning right, a fine walk across Chingford Plain to Queen Elizabeth's Lodge, the Royal Forest Hotel, and Chingford Station, whence you can catch (except evenings) a no. 397 bus back to Loughton.)

At the top of Rangers Road, cross the Epping New Road (again, being very careful), and enter the Forest by a stile about 25 yards north of the junction. (The stile was missing in late 2001) The path divides, and you should bear right. This area was cleared in 2001: it was formerly occupied by a dense stand of sweet chestnut, and regeneration of this persistent species can be expected.

To your right, you will see a clump of pines. Make for this clump by a side path. Pines are not, of course, native to the Forest, and these were planted when the owners of Warren Hill House enclosed the grounds. Just beyond the pines opens up one of Loughton's least known but most impressive views. Over the treetops on your left is the Roding Valley, the buildings "down below" obscured by trees. The vista is entirely rural, and extends from Chigwell to Hainault Forest. 100 yards further on, visible through a low fence (private, do not cross) is Warren Hill House, a superb Victorian Gothic mansion, built for the brewer, W H Sewell, occupied in Edwardian times by Sir Daniel Mackinnon Hamilton, and later by the Lusty family, who were the makers of Lloyd-loom woven furniture. It is now divided up into flats, and parts of the former grounds are Epping Forest buffer land.

Another criticism of the conservators was their shooting of so-called vermin. This is a humorous reflection on their persecution of the jay, still, happily, extant in Loughton.

Connaught Water from the west, looking towards Loughton and High Beech.

Retrace your steps to the pines, and turn right. This is a heath, with clumps of heather and many rabbits, which keep the sward short. Ahead is a fine oak, named Qvist's Oak in 2000, after the former Forest superintendent. It is unlopped, with an extensive canopy and a bole about 14ft in circumference. Join the ride, turning left by the oak, and descend the hill. You will see ahead of you the postbox at the top of Warren Hill, where the walk started.

Rabbit netting on the Forest, *Illustrated London News*, 9 October 1847. As its name implies, rabbit netting was carried on at the Warren, now the home of the Forest administration.

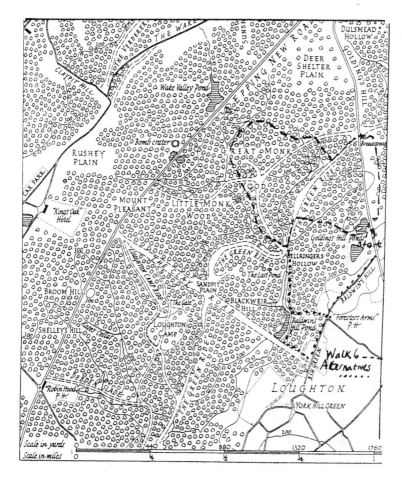

Walk 6

Walk 6
Great Monk Wood

- Start point: Goldings Hill Pond. Distance: 3.2 miles. Time, about 1hour 20 minutes. Terrain: The walk keeps generally to the 300ft contour, but because the area is intersected by valleys, there are several quite steep descents and climbs. There is one stream to be crossed, which requires average agility. Bus – 250 and H1 stop at the beginning of the walk and also at the Broadstrood Lodge end of it. Car parking – on street in Baldwins Hill. Refreshments: the Foresters' Arms, in Baldwins Hill.

We have left this furthest corner of Loughton's Forest to the last. James Brimble, author of the standard book on the Forest in the 1950s and 60s, would argue the best should always be left to last. Monk Wood is certainly rather different from the woodland to its south. Firstly, there are fewer pollard trees – it is not true there are none – and secondly, the land is high, and divided by the valleys of streams like the ribs of an umbrella. The woodland is more open than to the south, and the paths are rather less definite. This is a walk on which it easier to get lost than the preceding five. But there is no fear of actually losing your way. Each of the valleys, if you follow it downstream, leads to the one place, the head of Baldwins Hill Pond, and so you can always find your way back to the starting place.

Monk Wood, it is commonly alleged, remained immune from the Loughton practice of lopping because it was under the direct control of the abbot and monks of Waltham, hence its name. This, however, we find rather doubtful. The abbey of Waltham was dissolved in 1536, and the rights passed to lay lords of the manor, in the same way as the whole of the three manors of Debden, Alderton and Loughton, which make up the present parish. The Monk Woods were demesne land, rather than "waste" at the time of the survey of 1739. Whether the Lords of the Manor protected the Monk Woods more than the waste is uncertain, but another reason why lopping was not practised by the inhabitants in Monk Wood was probably simply its distance from the main settlement. After all, the lopwood had to be dragged laboriously by sledge off the Forest, and pulling a sledge up and down the valley sides, with or without horse power, for over two miles was not a task to be relished, or indeed, needed, when there was plenty of similar wood much nearer Loughton. And hornbeam, which burnt slowly and gave out a lot of heat, is not prevalent here as it was nearer Loughton.

Whatever the explanation, Monk Wood is certainly a superb piece of forest scenery.

Get off the bus at Goldings Hill Pond, or park the car just along Baldwins Hill from its junction with Goldings Hill. Walk along to the most southerly point of the pond. Goldings Hill Ponds, which were quite often regarded just as "Loughton Ponds", had their origin in watering horses and cooling wagon brakes, though there was probably gravel extraction there too. A ford through the upper pond allowed wagons to be driven through the water, so as to expand and cool the brake blocks before the long descent down Goldings Hill. A similar horse pond exists still at the foot of Buckhurst Hill, opposite Spring Grove.

The configuration of the ponds was changed in 2001, during de-silting and restoration operations, and as always after such work, they looked bare and derelict. Nature soon restores its own, and within a year, they will again be pretty and placid. Eutrophy – that is, the natural refilling of ponds by silt and driftwood, and their recolonisation with plants -- is a natural phenomenon, and every so often, re-digging has to be undertaken to keep them open.

Follow the southern boundary of the pond, and take the first path leading left from it, just by a very tall oak. The path descends through beeches, until you reach after about 350 yards the first stream. The stream is crossed by some logs round which the water flows, and the path rises through hornbeam and beech to come out onto the wide, surfaced Green Ride opposite a 9-trunked beech, regrowth round an ancient coppice stool. Turn left on to the Ride and follow it past a clearing where some recent pollards stand, some dead, until you come to a bridge. 20 yards beyond this first bridge is a path off to the right, just by a silver birch trunk that at some time has been cleanly snapped off about 12ft from the ground. If you continue along the Green Ride till you come to a pair of culverts, you have gone too far!

The path, which is unsurfaced, descends to two log bridges or culverts over two more of the Monk Wood steams, and then begins to climb, through beech, oak and birch, until you reach a very pleasant glade, with moss, bracken and coarse grasses. On your left, you will see an oak, which looks as if it had been recently pollarded, with regrowth perhaps a tenth as wide as the trunk about 10ft from the ground. In all probability, this resulted from wind damage, but the tree does give an idea of what most of Loughton's forest looked like 125 years ago. The old loppers would leave one bough on a beech to continue growth. If this is not done, the tree may die.

Enter the trees as the path goes through some rather boggy stretches (which are easily circumnavigated) and you come after a short distance to another oak and beech glade. At the end of this, the path crosses a large fallen beech, and you can see on your left another of the Monk Wood streams, this one being the Wake Valley stream, two arms of which descend from the area of the Epping New Road near Wake Valley Pond, on Loughton's north-western extremity. At this point the track becomes less marked, but keep right, and if there is a seeming choice of paths, choose the right hand one. You will now have been walking for about 50 minutes.

Keeping right, you descend to the valley of another stream. The path goes down to where it looks as if there should be a bridge – but in fact there is none. The stream, which is about 4ft wide, can however be crossed at several points where the banks open out. Resume the broad path the other side, which leads out to the Green Ride.

Here you have a choice. You can turn left, which brings you out in about 5 minutes to the Broadstrood car park in Goldings Hill. Here was once a pleasant keeper's lodge, built by Edmond Egan for J W Maitland when he was Lord of the Manor, for his keeper, Luffman, before the Corporation were appointed conservators. It was a half-timbered construction, unfortunately demolished in 1965.

Cross the main road, which can be very busy, into the car park, and turn immediately right, parallel to the A121, along an unsurfaced horse ride waymarked with white posts. In a few minutes, this leads down to the new keepers' cottages by the side of Gregson's Ride. Gregson was the owner and builder of Hartshill (walk 4), and it is said (we have never seen any evidence) that the ride was made to allow delivery of materials to the Hartshill site when the house was under construction.

Cross the road again, and walk back to the starting point, now in view. As you do so, you will pass on your right the 13th milestone, erected in the late 18th-century by the Epping and Ongar Turnpike Trust. This is a listed structure, without doubt the smallest in Epping Forest, and was maintained by the Loughton Town Council in 1998-99 along with the other two milestones in Loughton, one halfway down Church Hill, the other opposite Spring Grove.

If on rejoining the Green Ride you turn right, you can carry on to the point at which you left it, and having crossed the two culverts under the ride about 75 yards further on from where you originally turned right; strike out left by a path rising between the trees. This path follows the stream to Baldwins Hill Pond, and you can then cross the dam in front of it, and ascend the bank on its east side until you reach Baldwins Hill at the Foresters' Arms.

Loughton Ponds – *i.e.* Goldings Hill Pond.

FOILED! OR, THE FRIGHTFUL DEMON, THE FALSE WARDER, AND THE FAITHFUL CHAMPION.

A ROMANCE OF THE FOREST.

SCENE—*Epping Forest, in the Vicinity of High Beech.*

Enter CALIPASH.

Calipash (*striking an attitude*). I am the guardian of these sylvan
    shades,
These velvet sward-sweeps, and these verdant glades,
Oh, rather! Did not I announce last Autumn
That I in perpetuity had bought 'em,
Secured them for the PEOPLE? I'm the man
To play the pleasant part of Modern Pan.
Let trespassers bewar-r-re! Hollo! Who's this?

Enter Steam Demon, flourishing wildly.

Steam Demon. Snort! Squiggle! Squeal! Puff! Puff! Roar!
    Rattle! Hiss!
Calipash. Indeed! Your voice is really *very* pleasant,
    But I don't understand you quite—at present.
Steam Demon. I want free passage through these woods!
Calipash (*mincingly*).   *Proh pudor!*
    My duty's to be down on each intruder.
Steam Demon. I'm no intruder, I'm a boon-bestower,
    Friend of the proletariat Forest-goer.
    I've only thirteen Stations; want another.

The Frightful Demon, *Punch*, 24 March 1883. Drawn by Linley Sambourne. The
demon was the steam locomotive, when the Great Eastern Railway wanted to
extend its Chingford line into the Forest itself. The House of Commons had
debated and thrown out the GER (High Beech Extension) Bill on 12 March. Sir
Thomas Chambers MP stated that in 1877, the GER had wanted to build a loop
line between Chingford and Loughton. Such a line, in a deep cutting across the
ridge, would have destroyed the whole area of Walk 5.

A retrospect

We hope that you have enjoyed these walks in Loughton's Forest, and that they have whetted your appetite for more. There is no need to keep to them – you can wander anywhere and everywhere, and come across new glades and prospects. We have been walking in the Forest since we were children, and mainly in Loughton for the last 21 years since we came to live in Spring Grove. You do not tire of the Forest: it always gives you something new.

As you walk, salute the memory of Thomas Willingale, whose stubbornness proved the means of holding off the Forest's destruction, and of the Forest Fund, the Commons Society, people like Andrew Johnston and Edward North Buxton, and of course, the Corporation of London, who finished the job, and served notice that woodlands and open spaces were no longer fit only to be grubbed up and planted with corn, or houses, as Hainault Forest had been treated after 1851. If you ever walk or drive along Forest Road or New North Road in modern Hainault, look about you and reflect, for if it had not been for people such as these, such might be the current vista of Epping Forest too, and nowhere more than Loughton, whose Lord of the Manor was so intent on enclosure.

The conservationists won, and theirs were voices that influenced the whole ecological movement in Britain, and indeed, the world. And Loughton, in many ways, was the cradle of that movement. Let us 21st century Loughtonians never forget that, and – though the threat may be less distinct and not so wholesale – may we defend the Forest still.